LOVE
PANDEMIC

SALIMAH VALIANI

LOVE
PANDEMIC

POEMS
2022

Daraja Press

Published by
Daraja Press
https://darajapress.com

© 2022 Salimah Valiani

ISBN-13: 978-1-990263-53-8 (soft cover)
ISBN-13: 978-1-990263-47-7 (audiobook)

Cover art: Salimah Valiani
Cover design: Kate McDonnell

The following poems were published previously. 'On love (xxx)' was published in March 2020 by Praxis Magazine Online. 'Switch' was published in May 2020 by *Praxis Magazine Online*. 'Flip or, On love (xxxi)' was published in December 2020 in *Scarlett Leaf Review*. '1997' was published under the title 'Grandma' in *breathing for breadth* (TSAR 2005) by Salimah Valiani. 'Love Pandemic' was published in *Festival International de la Poesía Patria Grande Latinoamérica y el Caribe – We Are All One Todos somos uno*, in November 2021.

Library and Archives Canada Cataloguing in Publication
Title: Love pandemic : poems / Salimah Valiani.
Names: Valiani, Salimah, 1970- author.
Identifiers: Canadiana 20220283818 | ISBN 9781990263538 (softcover) Classification: LCC PS8643.A425 L68 2022 | DDC C811/.6—dc23

Dedication

for Dadima and Bapa, pathbreakers, lovers of poetry,
who passed while this collection was still in bud.

ACKNOWLEDGEMENTS

Love Pandemic is made up of yet more labour and thought than my previous collections. It was Andrea Meeson who suggested an audiobook, after receiving the first few voice note poems via WhatsApp in early 2020. Firoze Manji, publisher (and much else) of Daraja Press, graciously took up the idea, without a shred of funding to support the project. Maia Marie and Niel van Zyl lent me a professional recording device and meditation hut in the Magaliesburg Mountains and Maia guided me on how to make the recordings. Phumi, Maleeah and Ma were there all along. The editing and polishing work was done by Maia Marie and Sembene Manji. The constant feedback from my WhatsApp audience was another gift that brought these poems to bloom. All of this is a spiritual concretisation of love, at the heart of the collection. My profound thanks to all.

VIVA LOVE!

Contents

On love (xxx)

I begin nestled
in fluid   cord   organs

then skin and chests and breasts

I keep coming for limbs lips and cheeks

and when I'm full blown

I still need shoulders   hands and ears

my heart beats in yours

even if no one hears

even if this appears only through things
bought and sold

when I am told to self isolate

I will find my accordion   my tambourine   my
and play for you from my balcony

I will sing with you from my window

I will walk to your home   sms you to come out and
chat from 2 metres

I will forgo my work and play with you

I will find a way to give

in a world built and crumbling from
taking

1

deep
deeper
beyond
lightly floating
skimming
spicy
pulsating
twitching
extending
new
warm
heat-lined
flashing
sizzling
just plain hot
freeing
tickling
serene
lulling
sinking
bobbing

O

Mask

empty a two litre plastic bottle
take scissors to spout
split vertically
remove base and gnarly red-white label

cloak life-sapping with life-saving

never be deceived again

Rebellion

water heavier than oil that is hot
sinks to the bottom and is instantly heated
the resulting steam

blows the oil up

sugar on a grease fire creates the explosive force of dynamite

but then flour on a grease fire does the very same

Outward

hanging Grand-Bassam beds
chased up by corroding coasts

Antarctica glowing snow-green

unnamed bacteria and 330 Okavango carcasses

Inward

yellow fuchsia blue violet
cupcake heart butterfly

black mobile library
crimson Reading is Forever

almond-ochre-bead elephant

flying fire fish

magenta sky cubes

tawny turtles puzzling midnight guinea fowl

garlic-ginger owl

apricot aloes

bumblebee oriole

tangerine green sunflower

azul dreamcatcher

from colours inside Maleeah's bedroom

Switch

1
life matters after all

2
some lives are always expendable

1
health is a collective concern

3
force trumps care

15
no market without the majority (individuals ever-invisible)

22
the present is real but just a hitch in the road to the future

25
the power of non-human life
and domination still determinant

*

Ibn Sina
in a poem
taught of al-Arba'iniya: 40

quarantina   translated by Venetian merchants

40 days in the 11th century: not even 30 in the 21st

Flip
or, On love (xxxi)

Heads

desierto florido

200 flower species sheltered for years
until rare rain decrypts the seeds
for 10,000 desert blooms

*

Bombay pink: 150,000 flamingos foraging free

*

Outeniqua and Tsitsikamma

green purple yellow
green purple yellow
green purple yellow
green purple yellow

Tails

no answers no questions
just soldiers and police in streets and sheets

*

migrant rotis and
bones

strewn over rail lines

*

We are so hungry we could eat the crust from a wound

*

reclining
back turned to window
unable to hug and be hugged

Funerals   Sand

The new governor's words are orderly, clean,
inexhaustible, and cannot be told
one from another, like funerals, like sand.[1]

younger and younger mothers are dying of
HIV-AIDS   cancer   COVID-19

their very young kids prohibited
from burials
or not

...no rites in a gloom-filled room/Why cry for a soul set free
reads the funeral programme of a 29 year old niece in Katlehong

but we are crying for the body not the soul

the body   only now free of disease

in a section of a massive new cemetery serving three townships
18 piles of soil lay ready on a Friday
their message

this is the land you can have
and this is when you can have it

along the road there are
more seedlings than trees
their chorus

smoke of a snuffed candle
is little different
to steam rising from a bathtub
equal in length to a casket

The weight of height

the B&B owner picked me up at Graaff-Reinet bus station

at a tall lofty point in the centre of town she said

This is the most important point in town
If you get lost look up and you will get your bearings

that was the first time I noted the ominous tallness

in Robert Sobukwe's home-township
toward the top of the hill amidst unfinished RDP houses
the guide gestured to a point in the distance below saying

That was the pillar of Apartheid

his face fell
when I said my host told me

Never cross up into the hills

15 years on   walking Jozi's pandemic streets
those points appear everywhere
new ones daily it seems

I can't get my bearings in the histories of hate

1 Excerpt from 'The Song of Ptahhotep', *The Beauty of the Weapons: Selected Poems*
  1972-1982, by Robert Bringhurst (Copper Canyon Press: 1985).

for dadima

1997

bright yellow
dark red
green chilies turn my lips
hot red

bright yellow
dark red
no chilies or zest
in your hospital bed

bright yellow
dark red
a blanket of snow white
black boots I crunch through
you lose your mien
urine splashing free
you wait for the male nurse
grey in your dread

bright yellow
dark red
I cook and feed you
you taste and smile and
stop yourself short

to cook is a fabric of slippery silk pink
to eat is to frisk just a few of the threads
bright yellow
dark red
your torso
shudders cold
my arm nimble-green reaches for a blanket
faded
from washings with sterile blue soap

you smile a shade paler
cold and dark in your head

bright yellow
dark red
did you ever see my dadima?
you ask in a flash
bright passing memory   thought for the dead

bright yellow
dark red
a piece of skin
hangs
from the tip of your lip
I want
you want
to rip it from your grip
to quick tear it free

bright yellow   the urine
dark red   the blood
filling tubes poking in and out of you
dimming in a hospital bed

your colours and you
my colours and me

it's just you and yourself and myself and me

2019

porcelain mushrooms and trunk still solid

fading leaves banana-curled

what to do with a woman's pot-tree after she leaves home for a Home

water it with coffee dregs

hope that someone can do it again

2020

COVID killed our dadima
COVID   well   and

never knowing her mother
working from young
the arranged marriage
the divorce
the love marriage
the splintering

being independent in colonial Tanganyika

dislocation

centuries in the minority
and the minority in the minority

losing the freedom to
pray with the jamaat
cook
follow fancy
heartbreak of a broken hip

the final death   not COVID and dying alone
but three months of confusion
no family   no visits   no homemade food

to prevent the spread of COVID

but what made your 97 years live dadima

your wide open spirit

fearlessness to feel

creative hands working everything from cloth to pots plants to memory

your desire to know the world   ear to pulsing dilemmas

daily brandy and ginger ale   your full glass of gumption

conviction to choose despite being a girl child of the colonies

and your grand faith in Allah   strength of surrender

the way you kept on living and living with joy

long after you felt ready to go

I cut my hair when I heard
danced and danced to African guitars in Canada

the way your eyes drank green and purple rock patterns
we made on your gurney table
the last time we met

before your burial we will cook for you
picture you savouring
સેવ સોનચા કેસર આઢૂ લસણ ડુંગરી ડહી લીંબુ ચોખા

vitumbua I am suddenly craving

feast and a half in the triple distance

The distance of death

we cook this food you loved

pray on it   share it
together we eat this food

you will never eat again

du'a for the soul
flesh of collective feasting

Collateral COVID

progeny spread over 4 continents   6 countries   7 cities
no collective goodbye

gone the chance to mourn together   asperity
of a stretch of family history
one pandemic to another

novelty

out of nowhere shadowless splash of trunks leaves vines
out of the same nowhere
bird of a shape feather

never seen here

desire says enter
filigree fence of the air says look

don't touch

Love Pandemic

the heart has spilt all colours   many shades

from the spilling   words
from the swilling   countless acts

to inhabit the holes and transpose the whole

is to make love pandemic

On love (xxxii)

the octopus lives one year

tending in its three hearts and nine brains
the knowledge of forty million

years of changing colours
matching textures
travelling alone
emulating surroundings to

exist

toward the end of the year
if alive
the female octopus lays half a million eggs

with her three hearts and nine brains she begins a fast
measuring death in direct relation to (re)birth

erosion

if we don't meet again

remember I loved travelling
I will remember you did too

remember my dinner parties
I will remember you always arrived first

remember my jewellery
I will remember your close shave

remember I liked live concerts
I will remember you enjoyed clubbing

remember I finally took up sourdough
I will remember you disliked disguises and rigid rules

remember my smile
I will remember your tight rocking hug

Poetry titles from Daraja Press

A Mutiny of Morning • Nikesha Breeze

Nikesha Breeze has taken words from Joseph Conrad's *Heart of Darkness* and forced them to leave his colonized mind in a radical, surgical, and unapologetic Black appropriation. The resulting poems are sizzling purifications, violent restorations of integrity, pain, wound, bewilderment, rage, and sometimes luminous generosity.

ISBN-10: 1-990263-35-6 • ISBN-13: 978-1-990263-35-42
100 pages • $30 • https://bityl.co/DSZL

Love After Babel • Chandramohan S

*Winner of the Nicolás Cristóbal Guillén Batista Outstanding Book Award
from the Caribbean Philosophical Association*

Love after Babel deals with themes such as caste, the resistance of Dalit people, Dalit literature, islamophobia and other political themes, in almost one hundred poems. The introduction is by Suraj Yengde, award-winning scholar and activist from India.

ISBN-10: 1-988832-37-3 • ISBN-13: 978-1-988832-37-1
110 pages • $15.30 • https://bit.ly/3n9yNLr

Cradles • Salimah Valiani

Cradles is a collection of poems on the nature(s) and nurturing that cradle us. They are divided into four parts: Womb is the first cradle, both 'nature' and 'nurture', under-acknowledged and often unmentioned. Beyond the physical womb of individuals, there are collective wombs that incubate us on greater scales: lands, tides and winds.

ISBN-10: 0-995347-49-2 • ISBN 978-0-9953474-9-6
152 pages • $16 • https://bit.ly/3xgQo95

Poems for the Penniless • Issa G Shivji

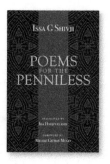

These poems by Issa Shivji, lawyer, activist and Tanzanian public intellectual, were written at different times in different circumstances. They give vent to personal anguish and political anger. Mostly were originally written in Kiswahili, here wonderfully translated by Ida Hadjivayanis, they are intensely personal and political.

ISBN-10: 1-988832-17-9 • ISBN-13: 978-1-988832-17-3
216 pages • $25 • https://bit.ly/3gue9Ve

Daraja Press

Order from **darajapress.com** or **zandgraphics.com**
Prices in U.S. dollars